12 S
Luxury Home Buyers Know That You Can Use Today

Jack Cotton

For Russell Fales

MY HIGH SCHOOL ENGLISH TEACHER

Copyright © 2010

Published in the United States by
Jack Cotton, CRS, CRB
851 Main Street
Osterville, MA 02655

All rights reserved. No part of this book may be reproduced in any form or by any means without prior written permission from the publisher except for brief quotations embodied in critical essay, article, or review. These articles and/or reviews must state the correct title and contributing authors of this book by name.
Cover design by Andrew Newman (www.newmandesign.com)

ISBN-978-1-60013-582-8

10 9 8 7 6 5 4 3 2 1

Acknowledgments

There are so many people without whom this book could not have been completed. I list them here with my heartfelt gratitude.

Melissa Rubinsky was immensely helpful in editing my first draft. Her questions forced me to clarify and explain things that seemed obvious to me but not to a reader.

Susan Kendrick of Write To Your Market was phenomenal in honing my title (www.writetoyourmarket.com), subtitle, and back cover copy. As usual, getting the words right on the back cover can be more of a challenge that writing the book itself.

I have not worked with a lot of editors, but still, I'm convinced that Barbara McNichol (www.BarbaraMcNichol.com) is one of the best. Her painstaking review of each word, her probing questions, and her rewrites have polished this book to perfection.

Much of the book was dictated into a digital recorder with a voice file e-mailed to Keith at eWord Solutions (www.eWordSolutions.com). Keith's team transcribes and turns around near-perfect Word documents, usually by the time the sun rises on the East Coast the following morning.

Thanks also go to Andrew Newman (www.newmandesign.com). Working from his low-key Cape Cod office, Andrew is a pleasure to work with and a true master of design.

Lastly, I want to express my gratitude for the love and support of my family including my four kids, Melissa, Andrew, Maxwell, and Alexa, and most of all my supportive wife, Ann Marie. Aside from being a great proofreader and sounding board, whenever she hears one of my ideas for a new project, she always says, "You can do that."

With heartfelt thanks and love, I express gratitude to all these people and especially to my family.

I began my Real Estate career in 1974 at the height of one of the worst Real Estate and economic crises in our country. Interest rates were in double digits, people waited in line on either odd or even days to get gasoline, and economic activity had nearly ground to a halt.

Since then, I've had the opportunity to work with thousands of people who have bought and sold real estate. I've dealt with everyone from hard-working people buying their first starter homes to corporate CEOs buying a seasonal home for eight figures they'll only use for eight weeks of the year.

As my career unfolded, I spent increasing amounts of time helping luxury home buyers and sellers with their Real Estate needs.

I have learned a lot from luxury home buyers in terms of how they approach the home-buying and ownership process. As you might expect, I've also gained valuable insight into the missteps people can make when they buy and own real estate.

Not Just Lottery Winners

In the Real Estate business, agents get to know all kinds of people during what is typically one of the most stressful times of their lives—when making probably the largest investment they'll ever make.

A few of the high-end people I've had the privilege to deal with reflect the profile of "the millionaire next door" that Drs. Thomas J. Stanley and William D. Danko describe in their book, *The Millionaire Next Door*. They profile the conservative, hard-working person who lives well within his or her means, and has quietly accumulated a net worth of more than a million dollars.

At the opposite end of the wealth spectrum is the person who has worked hard, founded a company, and then sold it for several hundred million dollars—sometimes even more than once.

At both ends of the spectrum are individuals who came into money suddenly through inheritance, lottery winnings, or some other means. Although you may love to be in this situation, you don't learn much from guessing the right number or being born well-off.

That's why this book was written. From it, you'll learn from those who made money the old-fashioned way—by earning it. Their "good luck" came from hard work and opportunity. This kind of luck is full of lessons from which we all can benefit.

After all, the "pure chance" kind of luck is just that: waiting for lightning to strike.

In thinking about everything I've learned dealing in luxury Real Estate over three and a half decades, I have put together twelve of the most critical "secrets" for you if you're considering buying real estate. I use the term *secrets* rather than strategies or techniques because, while they may seem like common sense, many have become lost over the years. These forgotten nuggets of knowledge will help you maximize your home-buying experience. More than that, you'll avoid the mistakes that so many people made in the past few years—people now suffering in the current depressed economy.

Think of these secrets as a best practices list from luxury home buyers. I'm not saying that all luxury home buyers use all twelve secrets consistently.

For example, some luxury home buyers choose not to work with experts in their real estate investments or get huge multimillion-dollar mortgages on their homes. From a Finance 101 standpoint, I understand the reasoning for leveraging your money; why not mortgage your home at 6 percent if you can earn 10 percent in some other investment. At the same time, in my thirty-six years in Real Estate, I have never seen someone get into trouble from having too little debt.

I've derived these secrets from my dealings with my entire luxury client base throughout the years. Think of this book as a "greatest hits" from my luxury home-buying clients. Many of these high-end buyers use them with "unconscious competence" meaning that they have become second nature to them. The action plan at the conclusion of each chapter will help you become "consciously competent" with these secrets.

Wisdom from a Mentor

I was fortunate when I began my career to have been around experienced people in business who had "seen it all."

One in particular started his career as a landscaper who, reportedly, had not attended school beyond the eighth grade. He cleared raw land for developers in the early days of his career.

Developers brought him onto a large tract of land to clear out the trees before the construction of roads and utilities. Because they couldn't afford to pay him for his hard work, they let him pick two or three choice building lots for himself. Over time, he became one of the largest property owners and the largest single property taxpayer in our town.

Financially conservative, my mentor believed that if you had to borrow to buy real estate, it should be paid off as quickly as possible. A child of the 1930s depression era, he saw what happened when people overextended and over-leveraged their money.

Everyone with any connection to Cape Cod Real Estate knew this man whom I met through my father. Several times during my budding career, I visited him at his home, often when I felt discouraged and on the verge of quitting Real Estate. He'd invariably tell me to get into his car and we'd drive past various homes, buildings, and tracts of land that would trigger hours of his storytelling about success, failure, and wisdom.

Today, I attribute much of my ability to navigate through difficult economic cycles—including the current economic low—to the "schooling" he impressed on me.

My mentor has long since passed away, but I still smile every time I think of him. I also say a prayer of gratitude for the wisdom and guidance I learned from him and others like him. They taught me to be conservative, to live within my means, and to make a plan to own real estate and own it free and clear—as I suggest to you throughout this book.

A luxury home-buyer's approach to the buying process differs greatly from that of most people. This is not solely because of the higher prices of the homes they buy, but also due to their overall mindset.

In these secrets, you'll learn (or re-learn) that they begin with a dream of their perfect home, whether it is a primary or vacation residence. They turn their dream into a goal and create a plan of action to attain it. On the other hand, many typical home buyers never even get past the dream stage.

You may think that the secrets you'll read about are not exactly secret. This may be true, but the main point I make in this book is this: these are secrets or principles that the luxury home buyer knows and *uses*.

That makes an enormous difference, I promise you!

Jack Cotton
May, 2010

Table of Contents

Secret #1: Luxury Home Buyers Dream—Big

Those who have reached the level of financial success that allows them to purchase a luxury home or estate know where it all begins—with a dream.

The wealthy actually "see" themselves in the mansion by the sea long before they ever live there. Chances are they "saw" themselves at the top of their field or career before they ever reached it. In the same way, they imagine themselves living in their new home.

How can one live a dream without first "seeing" or visualizing that dream?

Visualization

Websites, libraries and bookstores are great resources for books and articles that explain the importance of visualizing before you create and execute a plan required for achieving a big dream.

Start by creating a picture of the home you want to live in—and it doesn't have to be big. If you can't draw, and few of us can, look for pictures in magazines, books, Google searches, or just shoot your own photos of homes that appeal to you. In my early Real Estate days, I always carried a camera with me and took pictures of homes I liked and kept them in a file folder. This was before the days of hard drives.

Next, write a highly descriptive word picture of the home you would like to own. Load your description with detail: style, size, colors, setting, and more. Write your description in the present tense, as if you lived there already. Here is a sample:

I see myself coming home to a well maintained Cape Cod style home with two double windows on either side of the front door. There is a transom window above the door that is raised panel, naturally finished oak. To the right of the door is a hand-made, copper onion light.

There are easy-to-maintain and colorful planting beds around the front of the house and I can smell the Mayflower tree that is in full bloom by the corner of the house.

The naturally weathered gray cedar shingles soften the front elevation making my home look like part of the surroundings as if it were always here.

Inside, there is a foyer with naturally finished hard pine floors. There is a small closet to the left.

To the right is a living room with the same floors and a curved, brick fireplace in the corner. There is a picture window at the end of the room facing the side yard where there is a mature apple tree in full bloom.

At the back right corner of the house there is a formal dining room, same floors, and two built in corner cabinets for dishes and glasses.

To the left of the dining room is the kitchen with older but nicely maintained painted raised panel wood cabinets. I recently replaced the counter tops with granite the color of the sand on the beach I like to go to on weekends.

There is a hallway off of the bedroom with a full bath, and three bedrooms, the largest of which is in the back corner of the house and has its own bath. In addition, there are French doors that I added to access a small deck overlooking the back yard and a detached two-car garage.

When you offer valuable information in your marketing, EVERYONE has interest.

Put the following offer in all of your marketing: "Call and leave a voice mail with your name and address and we will send you a FREE copy of the newly published book ***12 Secrets Luxury Home Sellers (or Buyers) Know That YOU Can Use Today***. Learn the secrets of high end buyers and sellers. Limited supply, call today"

Each request for the book is a lead. Suggest they stop by your office or open house to pick up their copy.

Save $3.00 per book by ordering 10 copies for $169.00 with FREE shipping.

(MA Residents must add $10.56 Sales Tax Per Order)

Jack Cotton—Box 68—Osterville, MA 02655 Jack@Jackcotton.com t 508.776.0009 f 508 444.3309

How To Use The "Secrets Books" For Lead Generation

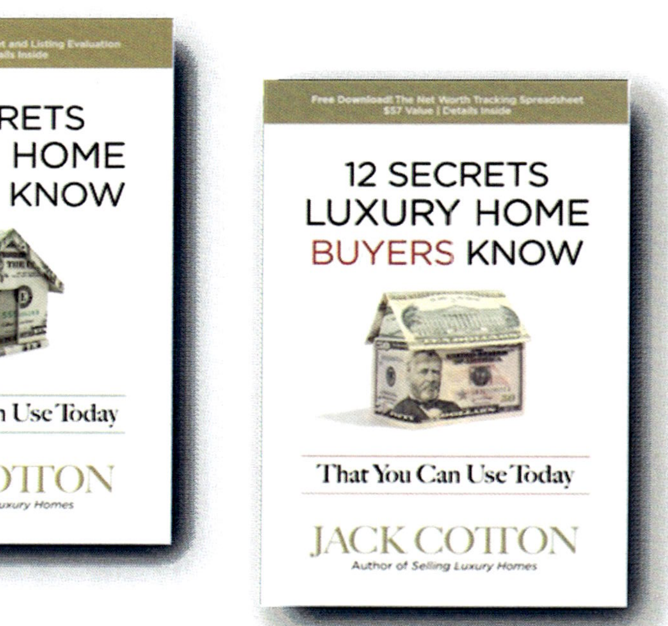

Whenever I return home after a hard day out in the world, my cares instantly leave me as I step inside. I can smell dinner cooking on the stainless steel range and know that an evening of quiet conversation awaits around the dining room table.

Grant's Dream Book

My daughter's high school friend Grant was an expert dreamer. While still in school, he created a "dream book" containing pictures of everything he wanted to achieve in life. With youthful enthusiasm, he included photos of mansions, boats, cars, and jets. Whatever luxury you can name, its image found a place in his dream book.

Grant carried around this book to reinforce his desire to achieve the dreams he portrayed. He even showed the book to select friends, thus making his commitment stronger. What better incentive for achieving your dreams than to solicit positive peer pressure like this?

Although I have lost track of this young man, my guess is that his life turned out well. Grant may even be living in the mansion today that he pictured in high school. You see, many of the luxury home buyers I've worked with took a similar approach to turning their big dreams into reality.

I especially enjoy curling up with a book by the side-yard-facing window where I can feel the outside to my left and see the fireplace at the opposite corner of the room.

All is well with the world when I am home.

I hope this gives you the idea. While it is easier for many to type this word picture into a computer, I recommend handwriting it first. I can't prove it, but I theorize that the magic of visualization works best with the kinetic connection that comes between writing hand and brain. You can always type it later on so it can be stored electronically.

You're about to make your own dream book.

Power of the Mind

Golfers know that when they tee off in front of a water hazard or sand trap and think about these obstacles too much, their balls are guaranteed to land in one of them. I remember mountain biking down a steep mountain trail in New Hampshire when a large rock appeared in front of me just as I rounded a bend. I had thought so much about the dire consequences of hitting the rock that, of course, my front tire hit it. Like the golfers driving balls into the hazards, what I focused on—hitting that rock—became real.

Maintaining that focus for the remainder of the ride, I managed to go over the handle bars two more times cracking ribs. Each trip over the bars reinforced the negative vision I had created.

Negative visions are hard to erase. I find it easier to replace them with new, more positive ones.

That's also why most of us can't walk a tightrope one hundred feet above the ground. We focus on the ground and it "gets real" in an unpleasant or even injurious way! Similarly, focusing on negative outcomes often becomes self-fulfilling—like my collision with the rock on the bike trail.

When you dare to dream big, describe your dream in words and pictures, and then put them in a readily accessible binder or on the hard drive of your computer, you're employing this principle of focus to your full advantage—in a positive way.

Again, I may be showing my age, but I prefer a small notebook that I can carry around rather than electronic files for my dream book. There is now software that allows you create a dream board screensaver for your computer. I have not tried this, but you might like to. Jack Canfield's website, www.JackCanfield.com, is one source of this software.

Get Started!

Start now to record your home-buying dreams—both verbally and visually. Gather photos of dining rooms, bedrooms, kitchens, and baths. For the outside of the house, include photos of the front, back, sides, even the roof. And if your dream is to have a garden, then fill a page with photos of a verdant, lush backyard.

What about your dream neighborhood? Include photos of parks, beaches, schools, and shopping areas in your dream book—the more detail the better. Remember, your goal is to represent in images everything you can so you can "see" your dream home as if it were already real. Even if you're starting out and your dream house is a cute bungalow and not a luxury mansion, begin "seeing" it now!

A Dream Come True

Growing up in my family's modest home, I'd often ride my bike around our village and gaze at the large homes near the water. One mansion especially caught the attention of my ten-year-old eyes, so I'd park my bike in front of it and dream, searing the image of this home into my brain.

Some twenty-five years later, I moved into that exact home. I remember standing on the front lawn with tears running down my face. I paused there and looked around for the boy on the bike parked on the other side of the Nantucket-style fence.

Those tears were not as big as the ones I shed when I sold it for a $300,000 loss a few years later in the great Real Estate meltdown of 1990 and 1991. Because my mortgage was small, the loss had no impact on my credit history, just my net worth.

Secret #1: Action Plan for Dreaming Big

- Start a dream book or dream file in your computer. In it, write a detailed description of the home you want to live in.
- Collect or take photos of homes that align with your description.
- Also collect or take photos of interiors, exteriors, gardens, neighborhoods, and other details about your dream home.
- Show others your dream book as a way to solidify your commitment to achieving your big dream.

Secret #2: Luxury Home Buyers Set Goals

Most of us tend to dream rather than set goals. Yes, we have big dreams, but then we just leave them at that—dreams—and say, "Someday I'll do that." Have you heard others—or even yourself—use the "someday" word? Lots of times?

Certainly most great accomplishments begin with a dream. At the same time, luxury home buyers know that to achieve something, a dream has to be upgraded to an actual goal. That's why they define a goal as a dream with a deadline.

Now, non-luxury buyers may know this, too, but the luxury home buyer methodically puts the dream into action.

Someday Isle

Imagine a ship's captain heading out on the seas with no timeline for reaching a specified destination. I wouldn't want to sail on that ship; it might never get there. (I guess it would be okay if my destination were Someday Isle!)

So if your goal is to own a home, then put a destination date on this dream. Will it be next month? Next year? Two years from now? If your answer is "someday," it will remain a dream, not a goal.

Select from Your Dream Book

Let's say you aim to own the home pictured in your dream book exactly one year from now. Take the page of the book that pictures your dream home and write the date you will own it below the photo. Congratulations. You have just turned your dream into a goal!

Next, as many times a day as you can, open and read your dream book or computer file, sharing it with significant people in your life. This helps internalize your goal of acquiring the home of your dreams.

Don't stop there. Post copies of the dated photo everywhere you will see them: in the bathroom, on the refrigerator door, in your work space, on your mirror, in your car, and so on.

Then on a blank page in your dream book or computer file, write down the following questions:

What will it feel like to wake up in this home?

What type of meal can I smell cooking on the stove, and how will this make me feel?

How will it feel to look out the window onto the backyard, deck, or patio?

What activities (e.g., remodeling, gardening, decorating) will I enjoy in this home, individually or with my family?

After a challenging day out in the world, how will my mood change when I see this home at the end of my commute?

Add similar questions on blank pages in your book.

Now for the Fun Part

Write out complete answers to all of your questions. These spell out the reasons you are absolutely committed to owning the home you have described.

Congratulations! You have just completed the first four steps in successful goal-setting. They are:

- Determine your goal.
- Write it down.
- Set a deadline date for achieving it.
- Write down why achieving this goal is important to you and your family.

More steps in this goal-setting process will unfold as you read more secrets. But you will realize that when you write things down, something magical happens.

Why Magic Happens When You Set Goals

Luxury home buyers use goal-setting in every aspect of their professional life, reviewing the goals they write down at least daily. Magic happens when people do this. Let me explain why.

A small area at the back of the human brain is called the reticular activating system, or RAS. Think of this system as a sensory filter that's needed because your brain simply can't process all the stimuli that assault it every second of the day.

Stimuli take the form of televisions and radios blaring, people talking, microwaves beeping, dogs barking, and even the sound of a passing siren at any moment. The RAS in your brain filters out what is not important to you so that what is important can enter your brain and be processed.

Think about a mother of a small child living in a city apartment. Day and night, they experience an auditory assault of noise: equipment grinding, horns blaring, sirens racing, aircraft flying overhead. Over time, her sensory filter—as well as that of her child—filters all this racket so both can sleep. But if the child makes the smallest noise in the dead of night, Mom wakes up with a start. Her RAS let through the sound that's most important to her.

Here's another example. Consider a time when you wanted to purchase a new car. Initially, you regarded the brand, model, and color as irrelevant. But what happened when you settled on buying a certain kind of car? Of course, you started seeing that brand, model, and color everywhere.

I can think of many times this happened, but none more memorable than the months after I ordered a Harley Davidson motorcycle.

After teaching a class in Luxury Home Marketing on Nantucket Island one perfect spring day, a group of us rented mopeds to tour around in the few hours we had before catching the ferry back to Cape Cod. We felt alive as we zipped along with the sky in its perfect shade of blue and the crisp, clean air around us.

The memory of this day clearly lingered in my psyche. Several days later, when I was returning from an appointment, my car made an involuntary right turn into the local Harley Davidson dealership.

My pulse quickened as I saw my reflection in the acres of polished chrome trim. My senses filled with the heady sensation of oiled leather as my hands ran across glided over the heavy stitching and stainless steel studs.

After I signed the purchase papers and began the several months of waiting until my Harley would arrive, I saw my exact big black Harley everywhere on the road. I'd never noticed any of them before! After all, my only two-wheel riding experience (except for my ten-speed as a kid) was on that moped in Nantucket.

If you've had a similar experience, you may be tempted to think, "Everyone is getting a Harley because I did. I'm a trendsetter." More likely, though, a highly anticipated purchase like this has programmed your RAS to process frequent appearances through this filter and into your brain. The object of your desire "registers" and you notice it repeatedly.

The luxury home buyer has learned to harness this phenomenon to his or her advantage in setting and achieving goals. Once the RAS is programmed by setting a particular goal, the outcome—along with all outside stimuli used to achieve that outcome—passes through this filter.

Similarly, as you become more focused on the details of your goal, you'll notice things that will help you achieve it. That's magic!

Secret #2: Action Plan

- Set your goal for buying a house, giving it a time deadline.
- Post copies of your dream house photo everywhere.
- Make your list of questions that address what's important to you (see list noted earlier) and write down your complete answers to each question.

Secret #3: Luxury Home Buyers Make a Financial Plan and Work It

Think back to the ship leaving its dock in Secret #2. The captain has set a goal, known in the rarified world of mariners as a destination.

Without naming a destination, setting a carefully charted course, and assigning a timeframe, how will the captain know where to go, how to get there, and when the ship will arrive?

Compare the dream of your home to a photo of the port of call you want to visit across the ocean. You envision the lush trees gently swaying against the azure sky, smell the warm salt-laced breeze, and feel the excitement that pervades the atmosphere. You intend to enjoy the adventure as you journey toward your destination.

The action plan you will create to achieve your goal is like the course the captain maps out for the trip. The captain takes the chart (nautical speak for map) and carefully plots a course from buoy to buoy across the water.

In this planning stage, the captain makes sure the course being charted avoids shoals, shallow areas, and other obstructions noted on the chart. The distance between each buoy or marker will be carefully measured with a scale found at the corner of the chart. Prevailing currents and likely winds and tides will also be noted. The captain will estimate the time required to travel between each buoy and then neatly mark the course and distance next to a pencil line drawn on the chart. When complete, the charted course will be, in essence, the captain's action plan to reach the desired destination.

To do what's required to embark on achieving your goal successfully, you need a similarly detailed plan of action.

As the captain begins the voyage, things change along the way. A later-than-planned departure might mean the tide or other current moves in an unexpected direction. The wind could kick up, making the journey rougher than predicted. Often on the ocean, floating obstacles, sudden fog, or other challenges require modifying the course of action.

So it is with your own action plan. Sometimes life gets in the way, forcing you to make mid-course corrections. There is nothing wrong with that. Indeed, the luxury home buyer knows that unexpected obstacles along the way often reveal unseen opportunities.

For example, few people are enjoying the economic climate that's plaguing the Real Estate business from 2008 through 2010 and perhaps beyond. Be assured that luxury home buyers know to look for opportunities. They'll most likely find them in high-value-for-the-dollar homes in unanticipated ways. They prove that often the best investments are made when everyone else is running the other way.

In any event, to luxury home buyers, this planning process isn't a secret; it's second nature—and in large part, it explains how most became wealthy in the first place.

Start with a Financial Plan

Over the years, I've learned that luxury home buyers, just like the ship's captain, know the type and location of the property they want, when they will buy it, how they will use it, how long they will use it, and how they will pay for it.

In particular, they know how they'll pay for their dream property because of their planning. Although the details vary, the important concept to remember here is that luxury home buyers *make a plan* for accomplishing the purchase. That plan includes reducing their risk and understanding their expenditures.

How to Reduce Your Risk

Luxury home buyers do not put themselves at risk to make a purchase. In most cases, they aim to avoid having to get outside financing. If they do use it, they view it as a temporary measure and always set a date on the calendar when the last loan payment will be made.

Taking a long-term view on property investment means luxury home purchasers obtain long-term fixed-rate financing with the intention to pay it off early. When they can pay it off (e.g., within five years when a company stock unlocks or when a bonus arrives), this results in short-term financing.

Let's say you've chosen to purchase your home exactly one year from now. What do you need to do in the next twelve months to prepare for that purchase? You'll likely have to gather funds for various expenses: down payment, closing costs, minor repairs, moving, and so on. This is where good planning comes in.

Say you need $20,000 for a down payment and closing costs but have saved only $8,000. You'll need to raise $12,000 in a year's time. How can you do it? It doesn't seem too tough when you break it down to $1,000 a month. Or does it?

How to Track Your Spending

I suggest emulating luxury home buyers by tracking your finances and especially your expenditures. You can be sure that luxury home buyers know their financial standing down to two decimal places. They know their net worth and they know what they can afford, both in terms of capital outlay to buy the home and cash outlay to maintain and run it.

Time-management trainers advocate their students write down everything they do with their time in six-minute increments over the course of a day. That's how they track how they spend their time. In fact, one of the coaches I have used over the years, Rich Rector, www.RichRector.com, had me keep a time journal for two months. At first it was tedious—writing down everything I did throughout the day.

At the end of each week, I had to fax my diary to Rich. You didn't want to have a call with Rich if the work was not done. It was highly illuminating to see how my time was spent—yes, even wasted—throughout the months.

You can do this, too, with your money. Here's how.

Start a financial journal to assess how you spend it. Use a little notebook, or a section of your dream book, or a computer program such as Excel or QuickBooks. Then write down everything you spend your money on throughout the day, every day. Total your expenditures at the end of the day, the week, and the month.

Put the following column headings on each page of your financial journal:

Date	**Description**	**Amount**	**Category**

Under the "Category" heading, create a list of items you typically spend cash on—lunch, coffee, bottled water, snacks, and taxis and note the date, description, and amount in each category.

Guess what you'll discover by tracking your money? You'll learn that little things add up fast—like that daily $3 cup of coffee. It's not a big deal at the point of purchase, but when your coffee purchases total between $50 and $60 at the end of the month, this becomes a big deal. And when you realize you've spent $600 at the end of the year, it's an even bigger deal.

Of course, it is easier to track expenses if you use a credit card. If your goal is to actually spend less, however, try to make all purchases in cash. It will take more effort to track expenditures as you will have to save, file, and record amounts and categories from receipts.

At the same time, spending with a credit card can seem rather painless as compared to actually counting out your cold, hard cash.

My ATM Habit

I tend to get my cash from ATMs that only dispense cash in $20 bills. So as I go through my day, it seems like anytime I buy something, I'm pulling a $20 bill from my wallet. Occasionally I get change back, but at the next point of purchase, I'm back to pulling out another $20 bill because I don't have enough change in my pocket to cover it. All of a sudden, the money is gone. Where did it go?

Because of this feeling of disappearing money and the ease of tracking my expenses, I use a credit or debit card for nearly all my purchases.

If you can discipline yourself to spend as little as possible, you can enjoy the convenience of having a credit card statement track your spending for you. However, if this approach causes you to spend more, then use cash.

How to Track Categories

If it makes sense for you, also use your credit card statement as a tracking tool. When reviewing my statement, I code every item with a category name including these:

- Rent
- Utilities
- Insurance
- Car payment
- Car repairs
- Fuel/Gas
- Food
- Clothing
- Entertainment

You get the idea. You'll find it's enlightening, indeed, to print off a detailed statement showing where your money went each month.

If you're diligent in your record-keeping, I guarantee you'll become diligent in your personal cost control. Spend only what is necessary and bank the rest for a down payment. Remember, that innocent $3 cup of coffee every workday adds up to $600 per year. It may not sound like much, but I'll bet you can find ten or so *other* purchases like that to cut back on or eliminate.

Remember, the less money you spend, the less money you need to borrow to buy a house. That's important because every $1,000 you borrow to buy a home can cost up to $3,000 throughout the life of the loan. That's comparable to buying a $1,000 audio system on your credit card that ends up costing almost $3,000 because of interest paid in carrying the loan.

I suggest you maintain a financial journal for at least one month and longer if you can. Applying the discipline of tracking will be a secondary benefit on top of revealing where the money went. If you're lucky, you'll turn this activity into a habit—as it is for most luxury home buyers.

Many luxury home buyers have actual family offices with staff people who pay bills and track expenses after shopping for the best deal. You can emulate this by using the suggestions and mindset above.

When using check writing expense tracking software, people who receive payment from you won't know if you have your own family office or staff person paying your bills for you! You will look that professional.

Keep Records for Your Loan Application

As part of your financial journal, keep a binder with copies of paid bills including those for utilities, rent, credit cards, and installment loans. Why is this? The more organized and complete the package you present to your mortgage lender, the more likely your application will be approved in a timely fashion.

Once you've pulled together your records, copy both sides of your cancelled checks from your bill payments, then staple them to the corresponding paid bill and neatly organize them by date.

Disciplined Approach Impresses!

An acquaintance told me about his buying a two-year-old car from a friend. The seller impressed him when he handed over a three-ring binder containing the complete maintenance records for the car. It included every oil change right down to the brand of oil and filter. It was astonishing that anyone would go into this much detail on the maintenance of a car.

The buyer found himself continuing this newly discovered discipline, tracking maintenance activities at the same level of detail the seller had. It turned out to be one of his favorite cars, and he put 300,000 miles on it before selling it for a profit. Without applying this level of discipline to maintain this car, it could have rusted away or fallen dead in the street before its time.

On separate sheets of paper or in Excel spreadsheets, organize and list all of your current bank accounts including checking, savings, IRAs, and other retirement accounts. Be sure to include the name, address, and phone number for each institution that holds your assets. If you are self-employed, include two years of tax returns in the package that you present to your mortgage lender. If you are an employee, put two years of pay stubs or W-2 forms in your mortgage application portfolio.

Create and Update Your Financial Statements

To keep following the secrets that high net worth individuals use in purchasing real estate, create a net worth statement and update it every six months.

When I was starting out, I maintained my net worth statement on the standard green ledger paper sold at the stationery store. It was exciting to see the amount of my net worth grow incrementally each month as I inched toward my goal. Doing this faithfully helps you track your ability to make and support a real estate purchase.

Figure 1 shows a sample net worth summary statement:

JACK COTTON LUXE

Net Worth Summary Page

Dewey Listem	as of	April 2, 2010

Total Liquid Assets	$135,250.00
Total Long-Term Assets	$350,000.00
Total Long-Term Debt	($98,500.00)
Net Worth	$386,750.00
Personal Property	$62,000.00
Personal Property Debt	($25,432.00)
Total Net Worth Plus Net Personal Property	$423,318.00

Figure 1.

Go to www.jackcotton.com and download the form for this net worth statement. You'll find a section for long-term assets (e.g., real estate and personal property such as cars and boats) plus a section for liquid assets (e.g., money market accounts and investments).

The data in Figure 1 summarizes information gleaned from Mr. Listem's financial situation. It includes liquid assets, long-term assets, personal property, and debts. On the form you can download from www.jackcotton.com, this data is summarized automatically from the separate pages or tabs in the spreadsheet.

You also want to create a liquid asset sheet that provides a record of all your bank accounts and investments. Figure 2 shows the Liquid Asset Sheet completed with sample data.

Liquid Assets as of April 02, 2010

Investment Type	Description	Institution	Account Number	Balance
money market account	personal	My Bank	123898	25,000.00
CD	Investment	Stocks R US	8372628	35,000.00
IRA	Retirement	Stocks R US	8383726	72,500.00
Now Checking Account	Cash	My Bank	9283736	2,750.00
Totals				**$135,250.00**

Figure 2.

Next, record your long-term assets. Typically, real estate is listed on its own sheet. Even if you have not yet purchased the property of your dreams, complete this sheet as if you already owned your dream house. That will give you the feel of what your financial situation would be once you have made the purchase.

The Long-Term Assets form in Figure 3 assumes that Mr. Listem inherited a duplex from his wealthy aunt, so you can see what the sheet looks like partially completed.

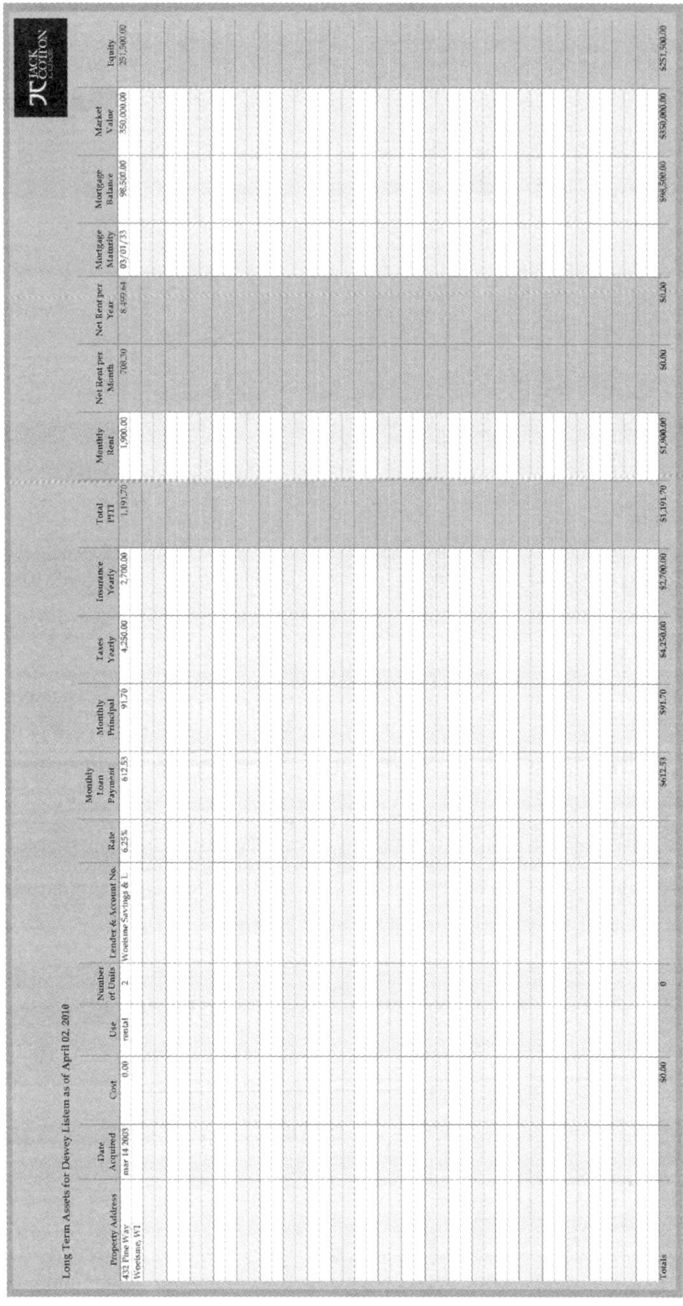

Long Term Assets for Dewey Listem as of April 02, 2010

Property Address	Date Acquired	Cost	Use	Number of Units	Lender & Account No.	Rate	Monthly Loan Payment	Monthly Principal	Taxes Yearly	Insurance Yearly	Total PITI	Monthly Rent	Net Rent per Month	Net Rent per Year	Mortgage Maturity	Mortgage Balance	Market Value	Equity
432 Pine Way Woeisme, WI	mar 14 2003	0.00	rental	2	Woeisme Savings & L	6.25%	612.53	91.70	4,250.00	2,700.00	1,191.70	1,900.00	708.30	8,499.64	03/01/33	98,500.00	350,000.00	251,500.00
Totals		$0.00		0			$612.53	$91.70	$4,250.00	$2,700.00	$1,191.70	$1,900.00	$0.00	$0.00		$98,500.00	$350,000.00	$251,500.00

Figure 3.

To complete your financial profile, compile a list of your personal property. While assets such as cars and boats are not considered investments, they are subject to liens and therefore should be listed in this financial profile. As you can see in Figure 4, Mr. Listem rarely resists buying "toys."

JACK COTTON

Personal Property Assets as of April 02, 2010

Property Type	Lien Holder	Lien Balance	Account Number	Monthly Payment	Current Value	Equity
2008 Chevy	Car Loans R Us	14,000.00	2828738	435.80	22,000.00	8,000.00
2005 Bass Boat	Boat Loans R US	11,432.00	837362910	355.86	15,000.00	3,568.00
Misc Furn & Jewelry	na	0.00	na	0.00	25,000.00	25,000.00
Totals		$25,432.00		$791.66	$62,000.00	$36,568.00

Figure 4.

Just as luxury home buyers do, know where you stand financially. You may be surprised when you see your finances organized on a spreadsheet; hopefully you look better than you thought you would be.

Your lender will be impressed when you hand over these completed spreadsheets. Update them at the end of each year and keep them on file so you can track your progress throughout the years.

Going the extra mile

If you want to take this exercise to the next level, take another blank net worth spreadsheet, date it for one year in the future and complete it, section by section, as you want it to appear on that date.

What do you want your liquid assets to look like? How much have you paid down on your various debts? What types of short-term assets are no longer on your statement and costing you cash flow to maintain?

This is a continuation of the visualization process we discussed in Chapter 1. Start another sheet dated five years out and another for ten years out. Keep them in your dream book or in that file on your hard drive so you can refer to them often, and make sure you are keeping on track. It is a lot of fun to track the progress to your financial goals.

Meet with a Lender

Next, make an appointment with a mortgage officer and complete a mortgage application. It not only provides practice, it's also a good way to gather information about how you'll be perceived as a purchaser in the marketplace.

As I mentioned earlier, many high net worth individuals are cash buyers of real estate. You, too, can be perceived as a "cash buyer" if you get pre-qualified by a lender before you start your property search. That way, you will know exactly how much you can support with your mortgage.

You might even consider buying a less expensive home than what you can actually afford. Luxury home buyers don't feel compelled to spend or invest the maximum they can afford. So if you pre-qualify for a $300,000 loan, don't rule out buying a home that requires a loan of $275,000 or less.

In more than three decades of dealing with wealthy luxury home buyers, I've seen how many of them got that way—by managing their funds with extreme care at every opportunity.

Many times we will have luxury home buyers who are new to our area buy a smaller or more modest home than they can afford to try out the area. Over time, as their finances improve and their commitment to the area increases, they will move up. I have seen some move up two to four times over a period of years to get to their final dream house.

More common is that at certain stages of their lives, wealthy home owners will scale back down to a smaller, easier to maintain residence. They can afford the help and staff to keep the residence going but don't like to waste the effort or finances.

Make an appointment, complete the application, and uncover any issues before they come up in an actual purchase situation. Then you can go out into the world of purchasing real estate as though you were a cash buyer.

Secret #3: Action Plan

- Create a financial journal to help you track your finances and plan for your future purchase.
- Discipline yourself to maintain the journal for a minimum of one month (much longer if you can).
- Gather the information required to create a net worth statement. Download a blank spreadsheet from www.jackcotton.com.
- Complete your net worth statement, list of liabilities, and financial profile.
- Complete net worth statements for one year, five years, and ten years into the future.
- Make an appointment with a mortgage professional to begin the process of applying for a mortgage.

Secret #4: Luxury Home Buyers Gather Data

Before luxury home buyers invest in anything, they conduct informal yet careful market research.

You can do the same. Look at locations in which you have an interest and see if prices are stable, increasing, or decreasing.

Research Prices

In what areas have prices decreased or increased the most? If one part of town shows home values decreasing more quickly than in others, investigate why. For example, on Cape Cod, homes in many golf course communities have been savagely hit by the Real Estate downturn, and the inventory of unsold homes continues to grow. At the same time, waterfront properties, especially those with piers that can accommodate boats in the forty- to fifty-foot range, remain in short supply and sales have not been hit hard at all.

Why the difference? Perhaps the local property tax structure is out of whack, services are poor, or schools are substandard. It could be for one key reason or several reasons, but it's *essential* for you to know what factors are affecting the prices. The more properties you investigate, the better idea you'll have of the values within the areas that interest you.

Research New Construction

Keep an eye out for new construction projects, whether undertaken privately or by local government. For example, you may notice that a town is building a large, new recreation center. While this may be regarded as a wonderful amenity, it could be a double-edged sword if the town has trouble supporting the added overhead this facility creates.

This could be a sign that property taxes will increase in the not-too-distant future.

Find out whether the project was financed through cash, bond issue, or another way. Ask how the town plans to maintain and run the facility. Do your research.

Private developments take the form of shopping centers, apartment buildings, or office parks. Look around and see if current similar facilities are fully rented or show signs of vacancy. Numerous "For Rent" signs mean that the business base of this particular area may not be as strong as it could be and that unemployment could be high. This could also have an adverse effect on the financial structure of the town.

Big Box Stores

On a recent drive home from New York City to Massachusetts, I was struck by the frequency and close spacing of large box stores along the highway. Does the local market really need a 60,000-square-foot electronics store every few miles? Clearly, commercial real estate gets overbuilt in some communities. Think carefully about buying a home in an area that has an unusually large amount of commercial vacancies. Many commercial vacancies can be a sign of high unemployment, which can be a sign of shaky city or town finances. Either can lead to eroding property values as municipal services get cut or eliminated and people move away.

Research School Rankings

Next, check the school rankings. A website search reveals various resources that can help you determine the ranking of public schools in terms of math and English proficiency. You can Google school rankings for your desired location or go to this site: www.psk12.com/rating/index.php.

In addition, check on the existence of high quality, reasonably priced private schools. They can have a positive influence on home values in a particular area.

Read ads and online listings for homes offered in your price range and/or preferred neighborhoods. And give yourself time! You can't decide one day to be a first-time home buyer and then buy a house the next.

Invest a good amount of time to study, become comfortable with, and understand the market. That includes building a price history of the areas where you are interested in living. Once you've settled on an area, learn everything that has occurred in that marketplace during the past year or so. Collect newspaper ads for homes and read the transfer directories often listed in the Real Estate section of the Sunday newspaper or in weekly newspapers. Find out how many homes have actually sold and what price they sold for. You can also search the online version of your local papers to find historical data.

Consumers can easily find offering prices of houses, but they rarely hear about actual selling prices. Everyone talks about "offering prices" and this is the number that is bandied about at cocktail parties and neighborhood gatherings. When the house finally sells, no one really keeps track of the final number unless they care to do the research. It is the offering price that is etched into the minds of neighbors. Of course, these two numbers can be vastly different. It's the selling price that matters most.

If you're a first-time home buyer, the most important number to know is what houses are typically selling for in the areas you want to live. Your Realtor®, whether a buyer's agent or a seller's agent, can provide information on recent sales from the online MLS (Multiple Listing Service). You can also visit REALTOR.com and other Real Estate data websites like Zillow.com to find information on recent comparable sales.

Once you have a solid base knowledge of offering prices and selling prices in your area of interest, you'll be an educated buyer who is ready to act.

Read a Book a Month

To assist in your studies, I suggest reading one finance or Real Estate book every month beginning now and continuing until you purchase a home. (You can find a list of my favorites in Appendix A.)

Think back to the methods you once learned in school to read quickly. Read the introduction, first and last chapters, and first and last paragraphs of all other chapters. Many business books feature bulleted items throughout. You can glean a lot of good information if you read only these.

Also note topics that interest you as you skim through the chapters. If something of importance stands out in a given chapter, read it all. Take your own notes and jot them down in the margins or on the blank pages found at end of most books. This will save the time of searching the entire book for points you want to refer to later.

Build a Network of Contacts

Luxury home buyers thrive on information. They know whom to call and what to ask to get the data they need quickly.

Peruse the local daily or weekly newspapers as well as websites that cover your desired neighborhood and discover the activities that exist and occur here. Are there parks, beaches, or other recreational facilities? How are they maintained? Do they attract like-minded people? Visit them at different times of the day to see how busy or noisy they are.

Also in the local papers, scour the Real Estate ads for homes for sale in your target area. Attend open houses and get a feel for what they sell for. Ask lots of questions.

More than from just a price standpoint, it's important to feel comfortable with the livability of neighborhoods where you may be interested in purchasing. I recommend that you visit the neighborhood at different times of the day and night to get a feel for the comings and goings. If you see lots of yellow crime scene tape, that's a bad sign. Are people driving fast on their way to and from work? Are homes neat and well maintained? Consider these factors about your potential future neighborhood as you build a reservoir of knowledge that will make you an educated purchaser.

I often advise home buyers that once they've narrowed down the neighborhood where they want to buy, they should knock on doors and ask the residents how they like living there. Have a friendly conversation and ask questions like these:

What do you like best and least about living in this neighborhood?

Is there anything you would change, such as a new playground or more shopping in close proximity, if you could?

Thinking of your neighbors, who do you suppose might sell their homes next?

Are you planning to move anytime soon?

The last two questions could give you first-hand knowledge of homes that may be coming on the market soon. Add your own questions and listen carefully. The demeanor and friendliness of the neighbors will tell you a lot about living there.

Of course be courteous, honest, and upfront about your reason for arriving at their doorsteps. I guarantee you'll learn a lot from doing this "up close and personal" research.

Secret #4: Action Plan

- Research your geographic area of interest to determine its livability:
- Find out about new construction and school rankings in this area.
- Make a list of people you "need to know" in this area.
- Talk to residents who live in your desired neighborhood.
- Tour the neighborhood in person at various times.
- At your local or online bookstore or library, choose the next five Real Estate or finance books you will read, and then read them!

Secret #5: Luxury Home Buyers Work with Experts

You might have gotten the impression that you'll be doing *all* of the research in your desired market area yourself and that you may even be spending copious amounts of time doing so.

Just know that this research process comes second nature to luxury home buyers who accomplish it quickly and subtly in the normal course of life. They don't make it a big job. Rather, they have made it a habit to ask questions of everyone they meet.

However, they also know the importance of working with professional experts.

You may be wondering, "Because I'm doing all this research and becoming an expert myself, do I really need a Real Estate agent?"

The luxury home buyer knows the answer is an unequivocal *yes*, so don't hesitate to interview two or three agents until you find one with whom you feel comfortable. Maybe you resonate with an agent who is assertive and offers definite opinions. Perhaps you prefer working with someone who's laid back and takes a counselor-like approach. Neither approach is right or wrong.

Remember, only you can decide what feels right for you. You'll be looking at numerous homes over a certain period and spending a lot of time with this person, so make sure you're both on the same page. Also make sure the agent listens to your concerns and clearly understands your needs and desires.

Think about it this way: Wealthy people are used to dealing with experts in all aspects of their lives. Whether they have medical, legal, or tax questions or needs, they have the ability to obtain the best guidance and expertise available—therefore they *expect* the best. Many times, this is a point of honor for them.

As an example, they love to know that their orthopedist treats the top performers on the local sports team or that their attorney wrote the law on a subject of mutual interest.

Wealthy people are used to—and will accept nothing but—the most expert practitioners in any field. The two-part question then becomes, "How do luxury home buyers *find* experts and how do they know someone actually *is* an expert?"

The answers are simple. They ask for recommendations from their friends and associates. They do online and local research to augment the recommendations from these sources. Most important, though, they rely on their ability to interview the recommended individual, either on the phone or in person, to glean important information.

In particular, as expert questioners and interviewers, "people of means" tend to have finely tuned BS detectors. You can develop a BS detector, too.

Here are questions to ask an agent before engaging his or her services:

How long have you been in business and what professional organizations do you belong to? While time spent in the Real Estate business is no guarantee of success, experience is certainly important. Membership in the National Association of REALTORS® and the affiliated CRS (Council of Residential Specialists) or CRB (Council of Real Estate Brokerage Managers) shows that your agent has a commitment to excellence and keeping up with changes in the Real Estate industry. Do you want an agent who is a full-time professional or would you be satisfied with a part-timer who has limited experience?

What professional designations have you earned? Did you know that more than two million people in the United States have a Real Estate license? Of these, well over one million belong to the National Association of Realtors®, which means they spend a significant amount of time in the business. Of all the Realtors® in the country, only a small percentage hold the Certified Residential Specialist (CRS) or Accredited Buyer Representative (ABR) designations. Agents who either have designations or are well on their way to obtaining one are the most professional and capable in the business. Ask what designations the prospective agent has and how it will help you in your search for a home.

May I have a copy of your résumé? Engaging a Real Estate agent to find a home is much like hiring a person to work for you. Would you conduct a job interview with someone who does not have a résumé? Do you really want to hire an agent who doesn't have enough pride in his or her qualifications and experience to submit them to you in writing?

How many hours a week do you spend previewing listings? You want to make sure that your agent has actually seen most of the homes he or she plans to present to you. You also want to know an agent's reasons for *not* submitting a particular home to you.

What kind of support staff do you have? Will I be interacting with them or with you primarily? The agent you hire should spend as much time as possible looking for homes that meet your needs. Filling out forms, writing ads, and chasing paperwork, while necessary work, takes away from time sifting through listing inventory for you.

How are you different from other agents in the area? Real Estate agents offer different levels of service. Ask your agent what makes him or her different from the pack. What can he or she offer you that others cannot? What are the most important "points of difference" to you?

May I have a copy of your buyer agency contract? You might also ask if you need to sign a contract at all. Some agents require this and others don't. If the agent you might hire requires one, read it carefully. Know your rights, what is expected of you, and what you can expect from the agent. Most important is to know the duration of the contract, the options you have to terminate the contract early, and what, if any, obligations you have if the contract expires or is canceled by either party.

Can you explain your policy on agency to me? Do you only work with buyers, sellers, or both? During your first appointment to talk about a specific property, your prospective Real Estate agent must explain agency laws to you and ask you to sign an agency disclosure form. Because you want to buy a home, you probably want an agent who will represent you as a "buyer agent." Your agent may also work with sellers, even the seller of the home you have interest in. There's nothing wrong with this. It is referred to as "dual agency" and is scary to some buyers. There is nothing wrong having an agent who represents both sides. You just need to be aware that it is occurring and acknowledge it in writing. Make sure you know how the "game" is being played.

How do you stay in tune with inventory in this market? Many homes are listed in the local MLS. Some homes, whether they are for sale by owners (FSBO), foreclosures, or builder homes, may not be listed in the MLS. Find out what resources your agent has to keep abreast of listings that are about to come on the market.

How quickly do you answer and respond to e-mails? Luxury home buyers are the type of people who stand in front of a microwave oven and yell, "Hurry up!" They want replies fast—in seconds. Most of all, they want to know what response time to expect.

Additional experts you'll need to source are an attorney, a lender, a home inspector, and in some states, a title company. Your agent can make recommendations for qualified experts in these fields. You can readily adapt this list of questions to any of these professions. And finding these experts will be the result of the same research you did to find your Real Estate agent. When you're satisfied with your search, add the agent to your list of referral sources for other experts you'll need in your home-buying journey.

Secret #5: Action Plan

Create your interview list of:

- Real Estate agents
- Lenders
- Attorneys
- Title companies
- Inspectors
- Compose your list of qualifying questions by adding to the ten questions outlined here.

Secret #6: Luxury Home Buyers Keep Their Ears to the Ground

Luxury home buyers seem to be the first to hear the inside or just breaking news and information from their desired markets.

I wish I had a dollar for every time a luxury home buyer with a connection to my market called me from somewhere in the world to confirm a new piece of information pertinent to this area—sometimes including information I had not yet heard even though I'm physically present.

One time I got a phone call from a European client. He asked me about the impending divorce of a couple who owned one of the premier properties in town. I had heard nothing about this even though I live right here. It's hard to compete with the "newsfeed" that luxury home buyers have. Still, you have to create your own version of it to keep abreast of all that's going on in your desired market area.

The foremost characteristic of luxury home buyers is that they like to be around people they know. They mingle with people who have the same goals, accomplishments, aspirations, and educational backgrounds. Typically, when they decide to buy a home—whether it's a first home, second home, or even a third home—the location isn't as important as how many people they know in a particular location. Rarely do high net worth individuals "parachute" into an area and buy a home where they have no personal connections.

That said, the first thing they do when they decide to buy in a particular market is to seek out, create, and tap into existing networks to find out:

- Who do I know already living there?

- How long have they been there?
- When did they buy their real estate?
- Did they make a good buy in terms of location, amenities, condition, and price?
- Who was the agent they worked with?

Litany of Questions

Whenever I spend any time with "people of means"—whether or not they're actively looking for property—I often come away exhausted from all the questions, as if I'd been given the third degree.

Listen to the litany of questions: "Well, Jack, what's the local market doing? How many homes are on the market now? How long does it take for them to sell? What kinds of buyers are coming in here? Are they new to the area, are they people with a connection, or are they the same people moving around? What do you think is happening on my street? What do you think about the tax situation?" Whew!

Sometimes, the questions come faster than I can respond because luxury home buyers are always gathering information. They ask these questions whether or not they are actively looking for real estate. They are always ready with a head full of useful, current market information.

I'm often amazed that people who have achieved such success would ask me questions about things related to real estate. Of course, I'm in the business, but sometimes I am amazed that people of this caliber are asking me for advice.

It proves that they not only crave information; they want that information confirmed and validated.

They use networks to keep abreast of market conditions, including how many homes are for sale, what's happening with prices, and what desirable properties are likely to come on the market next. They talk to different people with similar backgrounds and only make decisions after gathering lots and lots of valuable information. They've learned the fastest, most reliable way to obtain that information is through one's own network.

Work Your Networks

Not surprisingly, luxury home buyers use their networks for every aspect of their professional lives. Whether they're corporate CEOs or other highly compensated professionals or they're small business owners, their success came from working their spheres of influence. This is how they get referrals, build their businesses, and gain information about any market they plan to enter.

Working your network involves talking with every person you come across in your desired area. Ask what's going on, what's new, and what's changed. As you can imagine, luxury home buyers ask questions constantly.

Tap into Local Networks

To gather quality information about purchasing real estate, find a network of people you who live in the area where you want to move. Don't reinvent the wheel. Establish a network, keep your ears to the ground, and get all the information you can.

Looking Ahead

Think back to your school days when you were riding the bus home on the last day of school. Imagine yourself sitting on the bus with your final report card in your hand, not only wondering how you'll explain it to your parents, but also thinking about next year's teacher. You wonder, "What will that teacher be like?" Being curious, you looked for kids on the bus who were a grade or two ahead of you, who had already experienced that teacher. Then you asked questions to find out what kind of tests and homework you'd get and everything else you could expect from being in that teacher's class.

That's the same thing wealthy people do in all aspects of their lives. They look for people who have already been where they want to go and they ask incessant questions. When they're buying real estate, they tap into the local network and ask away.

Remember, an informed buyer makes better decisions than those who don't gather much information.

Be like luxury home buyers who keep their "radar" on when walking into a hardware store or a restaurant, or just meeting someone on the street. The questions continue: "How long have you lived here . . . what do you like about living here . . . who do you know who lives here . . . what don't you like about living here?"

High net worth individuals ask questions of everyone they converse with and then make their own decisions about the reliability and value of the answers they receive. They're on the lookout because they never know when that grain of truth or gem of information will turn up. As lifelong learners, they're always eager to discover something new.

Genuine Curiosity, Not Snobbery

A striking characteristic of luxury home buyers is that they never look down their noses at the person they're chatting with. As they ask questions and gather information, they respect the responses of everyone they encounter. In my experience, people *other* than the wealthy are more likely to have their noses in the air. They tend to say, "I won't ask that guy because he's just a landscaper," or "Why ask her; she's just a waitress?" In contrast, curious high-end home buyers ask *everyone* and then decide whether or not the information they get is usable.

When gathering information, luxury home buyers don't argue with their sources. They may test or play devil's advocate because they want to assess someone's level of certainty about what they are saying, but they don't protest it. They wouldn't risk interrupting the flow because they know information is money. Having the *right* information saves them time and helps avoid costly mistakes.

Secret #6: Action Plan

- Make a list of people you can add to your information-sharing network.
- Devise a plan for contacting them.
- Come up with questions you will ask them.
- Knowing that knowledge is king, gather as much information as you can from every source you encounter.
- Show respect to all who respond to your questions and don't argue with them.

Secret #7: Luxury Home Buyers Separate Emotion from Logic

The luxury home buyer has learned the value of separating emotion and logic.

To many, it would seem that investors would be all about logic and home buyers would be all about emotion, but what's true?

Those in sales know that people buy on emotion and justify their choices with fact. As someone who sells high-end real estate for second homes and retirement homes, I understand the value of selling to emotion. At the same time, high net worth individuals know how to separate the gut feelings from the equation and primarily make their decisions based on facts.

Emotions and Ego Don't Control Decisions

Of course, they have their emotional reasons for purchasing a home, but they *won't* make an emotional decision that will put them and their families at financial risk. They refuse to let their emotions or egos put them into an overextended position.

Yes, from high-end buyers I've learned that it's okay to let your emotions play a part in your decision to purchase real estate; just don't let them dominate your decision-making.

"Wannas" versus High-Enders

In many luxury market areas, I've identified a group of people I refer to as "Wannas." Often, they are service providers such as landscapers, contractors, and other professionals who cater to high-end home owners.

Day after day, they see their wealthy customers drive beautiful cars, live in opulent homes, and enjoy recreation in big boats. It's hard to see these luxuries "up front and personal" each day and not want them.

But while these Wannas may be doing okay financially, they lose their focus. Instead, they become preoccupied with not doing nearly as well as the wealthy people they serve. As much as they want to, they can't compete with these ultra-wealthy people in terms of lifestyle. Still, because they desire the nice house and car, they react emotionally and overextend themselves, rarely evaluating the financial consequences.

Although ultra-high net worth individuals might make purchase decisions from either an ego or emotional base, they remain highly aware of when they're indulging their emotion/ego versus *their ability to afford it.* They always mix in an underlying foundation of logic and fact. In contrast, many regular folks follow their emotions to make a purchase, and then use facts to justify those emotions.

Study the Situation

As they study the facts of the situation, they know a particular purchase won't overextend them and put their retirement or their children's education at risk. They also know this purchase won't jeopardize their family's well-being if disaster should strike.

In addition, compared to Wanna real estate purchasers, luxury home buyers *tend* to have less emotional commitment to the purchased property. They treat it with a degree of objectivity—more like a business transaction.

All told, high-end buyers don't necessarily make home purchases based on how they feel. If ego or emotion gets in the way, they know to adjust their approach and possibly move on to a different property.

To an outsider, their purchase decisions might appear impulsive because they can happen quickly. Yet I've witnessed their thorough thought processes. They've mentally surveyed their options twelve different ways before they step forward to make the purchase.

Base Your Decision on Fact

How can you emulate the luxury home buyer in making your purchase decision based on fact rather than emotion?

To begin with, review your answers to these questions from Secret #2:

What will the purchase of this home mean to me and my family?
What will it feel like to wake up in this home each morning?
What activities will I enjoy in this home individually and as a family?
How will I feel as I walk through the front door of my home after a tough day out in the world?

Were any of your answers emotional ones? They should be; their purpose was to create an emotional picture in your conscious and subconscious mind that will drive you toward your goal.

However, once you're ready to make an offer on your dream house, it's important to shift your focus to the facts surrounding the purchase. Yes, the emotional imagery at the beginning of the process helped you get to the point of affording this particular property. But now, put that aside. It's time to become the tough negotiator who will purchase at a price that makes sense for your financial situation.

Shift Your Mindset

Your mind-shift questions become:

What will the market support for a property like this?
What terms will I have to negotiate to finance the purchase?
What price can I afford, given these factors?

For example, let's say the market data supports $500,000 for the home you have your eye on. You can afford payments on a $450,000 mortgage as long as the rate goes no higher than 7 percent (one of the parameters that needs to be established to set your purchase limits). At this point, be sure to hold in check all your ego and emotional reasons for wanting this home. What is your maximum capacity to purchase this house?

Once luxury home buyers know their parameters, they rarely, if ever, invest at their maximum capacity to purchase. To imitate them, you'd reduce all of your figures by 5 to 10 percent to set your limits of how much you'll invest in a home.

That means you might set a maximum offering price of $450,000 to $475,000 for this home using the 5 to 10 percent parameters as a guide.

Again, luxury home buyers rarely invest at their maximum potential when purchasing a home. Of course, if you're looking in a market with a shortage of available homes and lots of competing buyers, you may have to go to the max. The point is, don't do it just because you can. If you have to go to your maximum potential purchase price, do it for the right reasons—the home is perfect for your family and nothing like it is currently on the market or likely to show up anytime soon.

The luxury home buyer knows that the real estate "opportunity of the century" will come up every month or so!

One More Piece of Advice

When you find a home that meets your needs and has an especially attractive price, find out how long it would take to sell the house if it were put on the market in two or three years.

Why is this important? Because it might be better to pay a little more for a quality house in a quality neighborhood than for a house that may be larger and more usable today but presents problems that could make it difficult to sell in the future.

Secret #7: Action Plan

For your dream house, determine your limits for:

- Price
- Monthly payments
- Maintenance costs
- Improvement costs

Reduce all these figures by 5 to 10 percent to set your parameters for your maximum purchase price.

Luxury home buyers understand finance and financing and have mastered the concept of the time value of money.

In speeches and training classes, I conduct for Real Estate agents, I often quote Albert Einstein who said that compound interest should be the eighth wonder of the world.

Interest is, of course, the money you earn on your money you have invested and conversely, the money you pay on money you borrow.

If you put $100 in the bank today at 5 percent interest, you would have $105 at the end of the year if the interest is compounded yearly. The second year, you earn the 5 percent on both the original $100 as well as on the $5 you earned last year and left in the account. Therefore, instead of earning $5 the next year, you earn 5 percent on $105, which yields $110.25.

In the real world, interest you earn and pay is compounded continuously. This means you would actually have $105.12 in the account at the end of year one.

Your money will double in about fifteen years if it earns 5 percent, and in only ten years at 8 percent.

Unfortunately, the same holds true when you borrow money. Let's say you spend $100 on your credit card and take three years to pay it off. Credit card interest is much higher that savings interest and can approach 18 percent and more. The amount you paid in total at the end of three years for that $100 item is $170.91. What this means is that the

$100 dinner you charged on your credit card could really be costing you quite a bit more than you thought.

It is more fun to think about the "wonder" of compound interest from a savings or investment standpoint. Putting $100 per month away into a savings account that earns an average of 5 percent would grow to more than $15,528 during ten years and $41,103 in twenty years.

Luxury home buyers understand this as well as knowing what they can afford. They won't let a particular real estate purchase "strap" them or jeopardize their family's future, as noted in Secret #7.

You'd learn from them by understanding your own finances with your net worth statement and financial diary (as discussed in Secret #3). Then you'd take the snapshot you created of your financial picture to the next level by learning how others, especially lenders, are likely to view it.

Begin that process by ordering a copy of your credit report from the three main reporting agencies lenders rely on, Experian®, Equifax® and TransUnion®.

These competitors gather their information in different ways and therefore may show different ratings for you. This is especially true if one of the agencies made an error in collecting your financial data.

Because you don't know which of these reporting agencies your lender will use, it's best to check your report with all three.

When you're ready to buy, your lender will look at your credit score to predict your financial strength in the same way the meteorologist looks at the barometer to get a picture of the weather. In both cases, they aren't "looking out the window" at what's nearby to gain information.

Gone are "Looking Out the Window" Days

How often do you wish the weather reporter would just look out the window for current information? Many are the days here on Cape Cod when the weather report calls for sunshine but we're dodging raindrops.

In the old days, lenders did "look out the window" to gauge your credit worthiness as a borrower. They sat across from you at a big desk in a big chair while you sweated away in a much lower chair. The lending officer would look at your statement quickly, but would base the decision to lend on his or her "feel" of you as a credit risk.

You can kiss those days goodbye. Today, you're regarded as a number, and that number is your credit score. It reveals how those who will say yes or no to your application will view you.

Despite your charm and wit, I can assure you, lenders will see you as that number. That's why you need to know what it is, and if it's not a high score, take action to increase it before you sit down to complete a mortgage application.

How to Improve Your Credit Score

Start by studying books and reputable websites on how to improve your credit score, and if I were to write one, I'd include these three main steps:

1. Federal law allows you to receive a free copy of your credit report once every twelve months. You can order your own summary of all three reports at www.annualcreditreport.com. Completing the application found at this site, you will receive a credit report from all three agencies. After receiving your credit reports, examine them meticulously to check for errors. This is the most common and theoretically easy "fix" to accomplish. Possible errors include accounts shown as open that have been closed, incorrect balances or actions on a particular account, or payments incorrectly listed as late.

2. Don't cancel any existing credit cards because this will adversely affect your score. Do your best to pay them off each month, starting with the account that has the smallest balance. While it is financially better to pay off debt with the highest interest first, you have to consider the trade-off with the progress you will feel as one card or debt is totally paid off.

    a. As each of your debts get paid off, your monthly payment will, of course, decrease. Rather than spending this money, keep making the same payment toward other debts you have and they will shrink even faster.

    b. Put the eighth wonder of the world to work for you.

    c. Don't charge up to the limit on any account. The longer your record of underutilizing your total available credit, the better. If you plan to purchase a house soon, don't buy any other items unless you pay cash for them in full. Multiple inquiries by creditors on your credit history can lower your score.

3. Write to any banks or entities that have extended you credit and request they remove any late payments shown on your report if possible. The best action is to pay all bills early, or at the very least, on time. Unfortunately, years of consistently timed payments can be ruined quickly with a low number of late payments.

To understand what's on a credit report, review the sample from Experian that can be found at www.Experion.com.

Your credit score (also known as a FICO score after the company Fair Isaac Corporation that developed this scoring system) is a number between 300 and 900. The higher the score, the better. Most people fall into the 600 to 700 range.

Not only does having a high score result in a lower interest rate, it might also be the difference between getting approved or not. Gone are the days of being approved for a loan as long as you can fog a mirror.

Pay Bills On (or Before) Due Dates

When many people receive their utility, rent, or car payment bill, they note two things: the due date and the "late if not paid by date."

If a bill is due on the first of the month and there is a penalty for payment after the 15th, many people think it's okay to pay it on or before the 15th.

Well, it's not. The bill is due when the bill is due, which is on the first, so that's when you should pay it. In fact, to be sure it's noted as paid on time, send the payment early enough to ensure it arrives a few days *ahead* of the due date. If you pay bills to the same creditor every thirty days, just send your check early; your payments will still be thirty days apart. The luxury home buyer prefers to pay bills early in the cycle rather than toward the end of the thirty days.

Make sure that your total payments for all debt including mortgage payment (or rent payment, if you don't own real estate), car payment, credit card payments (if not paid in full each month), and all other loan payments together total less than 30 percent of your income.

Pay yourself first

Most people earn their salary, pay their expenses, and have nothing left at the end of the month. Even when they get a raise, their expenses "grow into" their new paycheck and there is still nothing left at the end of the month.

The luxury home buyer always pays himself or herself first. I remember when I first heard this concept from my friend and Real

Estate speaker, Howard Brinton. I thought he was crazy when I first heard it. I was one of those who put into savings or investments the leftovers. Usually there was not much left over.

Howard taught his loyal followers to take a minimum of 10 percent of their pay "off the top." Pretend they never got it, and salt it away. Pay your bills and expenses with the other 90 percent and live within those means.

Many luxury home buyers pay themselves first at levels even higher than 10 percent. Imagine if the $100 per month we discussed a few paragraphs earlier became $100 per week, for example. At 5 percent interest, you would have saved over $165,000 at the end of ten years.

Pre-Qualify for Your Mortgage

Because most people can't pay cash for a real estate purchase, preparing for and meeting with a mortgage lender to get "pre-approved" status allows them to make an offer on a home. If you have a pre-approval letter in hand, you essentially become a cash buyer.

When you meet with the mortgage officers (as discussed in Secret #3), you display your portfolio of financial information including copies of both sides of your cancelled checks for bill payments. This shows the lending officers and underwriters how close to due dates you have been paying other bills, thus indicating how you are likely to handle your mortgage payment.

Getting pre-qualified means that the lending officer, after reviewing your financial data, is comfortable determining how much mortgage you can afford. That amount indicates what house price you can afford, which takes the process one step closer to completion.

Being pre-approved is one step better than being pre-qualified. Getting pre-qualified means that if everything you've submitted to the lender is true, you will qualify for the loan. Getting pre-approved means the lender has verified your credit history and actually approved you for receiving financing. At that point, all that remains is to find the property you plan to purchase and have it appraise for what you want to pay for it.

The pre-approval process handles all the credit checking and underwriting as though you were actually applying for a loan. Once you are pre-approved, the only thing left in securing a mortgage is to find the house you want to purchase.

Once you're pre-approved and ready to make an offer on a home, attach a copy of your pre-approval letter with your written offer. What's the advantage of doing that? If there are multiple offers on the house of your dreams, your offer will look more attractive than others because your ability to get a mortgage has been fully approved.

One tip here is to ask your lender for two pre-approval letters. One will state the amount for which you are pre-approved to borrow. The second should say something like, "John and Jane Dow are approved for the mortgage they are seeking."

This way, when you submit the letter with your offer, the seller will not know the amount for which you are approved. It can help your bargaining position if you are starting with a low offer. Do you really want the seller to know the amount you are approved for?

Start "Paying" the Mortgage Amount Now

If you're renting your residence now and want to emulate people in the high end, *pretend* you have a mortgage.

That's right. Say you pay $1,300 a month and that the mortgage payment on your dream home will be $1,600 a month. Start making the $1,600 monthly payment as if you already own the house. Pay the $1,300 to your landlord and put the other $300 into a savings account. If you practice paying the mortgage amount and bank the difference, you're doing what those in the high-end market would do.

Tempting Investment Options

I hear time and again, especially from mortgage lenders and investment advisors, that a winning strategy is to finance your residence at 5 or 6 percent and then invest in the market to earn a return of 12 percent. If you can make this happen, they say, you'd be crazy to pay cash for your real estate.

However, here's my experience: Luxury home buyers might employ this strategy with real estate they own for investment, but not with the real estate they live in. There are homes on the market today whose owners borrowed money with a 6 percent mortgage because they had been quoted a rate of return twice that amount—12 percent—by their investment advisor. But what happens when the investment advisor turns out to be a scammer? Does the name Bernie Madoff ring a bell?

Of course, you don't need to have invested with a scammer to lose money on your investments. Look at the way many stock market portfolios performed from a market peak in October of 2007 to the spring of 2009 when the Standard and Poor's 500 Index dropped more than 50 percent. Imagine having borrowed a large amount against the equity in your home so you could invest the money in the market during that time.

Let's say you had a $200,000 home with no mortgage. You have, therefore, $200,000 in equity in your home. Against that equity, you borrowed $100,000 to invest in the stock market. Suppose that same $100,000 you invested is now worth around $50,000 due to gyrations in the market or just plain bad stock picking. And if your home value dropped by 30 percent—and homes values did in many areas of the country—your $200,000 home has become worth $140,000. This means your equity (calculated by subtracting the loan amount from the market value) has dropped from $100,000 to $40,000. Talk about a bad year. You also still have $50,000 left in the stock market, unless of course you invested with a crook, which some people did.

Don't Mess with Your Main Home

Your residence is the cornerstone of your financial life, the foundation of your family life, which is why I suggest paying off this debt as soon as you possibly can. Most luxury home buyers don't care if they can earn three times the interest rate in the stock market; they simply don't leverage the homes they live in, whether it's their primary or vacation home.

As an exception, *if* you can get a good deal on a real estate purchase today and *if* your stock options can be cashed out in twelve or eighteen months, you might want to take a short-term mortgage.

Another exception is the luxury home buyer who might purchase an apartment complex leveraged in a way that the rent covers the mortgage and expenses, thus preserving capital that can be deployed at a higher rate. This type of leverage *can* make sense because it's not leveraging the dwelling where the family resides.

Pay Off Mortgage Early

Home purchasers may not be in the financial position to pay cash or borrow short-term to make the transaction; however, every home buyer *can* make and execute a plan to accelerate his or her mortgage payments. The goal: to pay off the home in ten to fifteen years rather than thirty. Every extra dollar you pay toward the principal of your home loan early on can save *two to three dollars* in interest throughout the life of the loan, depending on the interest rate.

After suffering one of my famous stock market losses about six years ago, I told my wife the only way I knew to earn a guaranteed 6 percent return on our money was to pay off our home mortgage. We did and I'm glad we did. It's no fun to lose money on an investment knowing that you could have earned a substantial return with a "sure thing"—paying down your mortgage.

Buy a House Worth Less Than Your Max

The luxury home buyer knows that if you need to buy less house, you buy less house. That means if you can afford a million-dollar house, buy a $700,000 house instead. If you can afford a $500,000 house, then buy a $350,000 house instead.

Too many people used the easy money available in 2004 through 2006 to buy a more sizable house than they could afford. After all, they reasoned, home prices had never gone down on a nationwide basis since the day the record-keeping started. Many of these buyers expected that trend to continue forever.

Buying a home that costs less than the maximum you've determined you can afford allows you to afford improvements if the home doesn't have everything you want. For example, if you want to upgrade a kitchen or a bathroom or add on a family room, you'd take that into consideration when making the purchase.

Create a long-term calendar to plan when you will make certain improvements and repairs, and decide how you will fund them. Preferably, you will not finance the work by refinancing or getting a second mortgage on the house!

Look at these scenarios: A $100,000 mortgage at 5 percent for thirty years costs $536.82 a month. The same loan for twenty years costs $659.96 a month, and for fifteen years costs $790.79 a month.

Many people say, "I can't spend an extra $253.97 on my mortgage every month!" The luxury home buyer understands that one is not "spending" this extra money each month. Yes, the check is made payable to the mortgage lender, but 100 percent of the extra payment is going toward the principal of the loan. That means it goes into the equity of your house, so you're *not spending* it; you're *saving* it.

You will indeed make a higher payment each month, but at the end of fifteen years, the loan will be paid off and you will have paid $50,913 *less* in interest.

Your parents and grandparents probably told you that the only mortgage to get is a twenty- or thirty-year fixed-rate loan. That's how they did it, and that's how they say you should do it, too. But previous generations often lived in their homes for decades. Your generation moves around a lot more.

Tax Deduction Not a Big Advantage

Check with tax laws in your state to see if home interest is deductible on your state tax return. In Massachusetts, for example, home interest is not deductible on one's state tax return.

You may assume that home interest is totally deductible on one's federal tax return, but that's not true. I talked with CPA Janet Feeney of DePaola Begg, an accounting firm in Hyannis, Massachusetts, about the home mortgage interest deduction. She spelled out three categories of mortgage debt to consider.

The first is grandfathered debt, which includes mortgages taken out before October 13, 1987. All of the interest paid on grandfathered debt is fully deductible as home mortgage interest.

The second category is acquisition debt—a mortgage or home equity loan used to actually purchase, build, or substantially improve your home. The total debt that can be treated as acquisition debt is one million dollars ($500,000 if married filing separately). This means that the interest on the first million dollars of acquisition debt may be deductible on your federal return. So if you had two million dollars of acquisition debt, your home mortgage interest deduction would be limited to the interest on one million. Debt over this limit may qualify as home equity debt, the third category.

Lastly, there is home equity debt, which is debt secured by your home, the proceeds of which were not used to purchase, build, or substantially improve it. Examples would be debt incurred for college tuition, purchasing a car, or going on an around-the-world vacation. The limit on the amount of debt that can be treated as home equity debt is the smaller of $100,000 or the fair market value of your home, reduced by any home acquisition debt and grandfathered debt. You cannot deduct the interest on debt that exceeds this limit as home mortgage interest.

If this isn't complicated enough, you may not be aware that, on home equity indebtedness up to $100,000, the interest you may have deducted on this debt must be added back when you are subject to the Alternative Minimum Tax or AMT.

Understand that this book isn't intended to give tax advice. Please seek competent advice from a tax professional who understands your circumstances. The point I want to make here is this: you have no tax-related reason to maintain a mortgage on your home.

Short-Term vs. Long-Term Loans

In today's loan climate, you will pay a higher rate of interest for a twenty- or thirty-year fixed-rate mortgage than for a short-term adjustable-rate mortgage. So if you're likely to live in your house for only three to five years, perhaps it makes more sense to get a three- or five-year adjustable-rate mortgage.

Your plans can change, though, and if they do, having a fixed-rate long-term mortgage does provide added security against rate hikes.

Here's an example: A thirty-year $100,000 mortgage with a fixed rate of 6 percent will cost just about $600 per month, while a three-year adjustable loan with a rate of 7.5 percent after a rate increase will cost nearly $700 per month. The monthly savings of about $100 amounts to $1,200 per year. Impressive!

If your adjustable rate mortgage continues to adjust upward, the savings from a fixed-rate mortgage only increase.

You may believe you won't stay in your house for thirty years—that you'll change in three to five years—and so you'll be tempted by the lower rate. But learn from the luxury home buyer who locks in favorable rates for as long as possible, whether it is a favorable low rate on a mortgage or a favorable high rate on an investment.

Secret #8: Action Plan

- To find out your credit score, order credit reports from one or all of these vendors:

  Experian® www.experian.com
  Equifax® www.equifax.com
  TransUnion® www.transunion.com
- If your score is low, take action to improve it.
- Have preliminary meetings with lenders to determine your creditworthiness with them.
- Take steps to pre-qualify (e.g., make sure your financial portfolio is up to date and credit score is good).
- Choose your payment options wisely; don't overextend yourself or listen to advisors who recommend investments that seem too good to be true—because they probably are.
- Aim to pay down your mortgage early.
- Lock in the most favorable loan rate for your circumstances.

Secret #9: Luxury Home Buyers Know the Importance of Equity

When luxury home buyers purchase real estate, they know they can both protect the property's value and increase it. How? By maintaining the systems and structure of the house in an organized, preemptive manner.

This starts from understanding exactly what they're getting into from a maintenance and upkeep standpoint. This aspect is just as critical as understanding the mortgage and investment side of the purchase. They don't simply buy a property and leave themselves open to constant maintenance surprises.

Do Thorough Research Before Buying

Before they buy, high-end buyers do thorough research. They have qualified people go through and inspect the property so they know what to expect. If told they'll need a new roof in three years, they don't just say, "Well, what the heck, I'll worry about it in three years." They plan for it at the time of the purchase. How? Either by negotiating a better price, by putting money aside, or by passing on that property and looking for one that doesn't require a new roof that soon.

In contrast, a typical home buyer calls in Uncle Fred or a teammate from their bowling league to serve as their advisor, or worse, as their inspector. The luxury home buyer knows the importance of having *qualified* people do the research, not buddies who may be willing to help but aren't professionals in home inspection.

Keep Home in Ready-to-Sell-Fast Shape

Once luxury home buyers purchase a property, they carefully maintain it in such a way that it would be ready to go on the market tomorrow, even though they have no intention of selling it right away.

There is always a plan for maintaining the property, the grounds, and the systems. They make sure the property is in good condition—painted, clean, and well-tuned. Only rarely does someone in the high-end market buy a property and then let it fall into disrepair. Rather, they know exactly what it will take to maintain it and take measures right away such as hiring gardeners and handymen. They also make sure they have money available to underwrite maintenance and manpower costs, including a management company or a full-time caretaker. They want to keep the property in perfect condition so any time they decide to use it or sell it, it's ready.

Wealthy people know that whatever the purchase—a house, plane, car, boat—they need funds to maintain it. Having a boat, for example, can cost 20 percent of the purchase price per year to maintain, and airplanes cost more than that.

Ownership Process: A Journey, not a Destination

Many buyers in the lower price ranges view a purchase as a destination, thinking, "Once I acquire this house, everything is going to be great. I can just move in and enjoy it."

But high net worth buyers look at a purchase as a journey, not a destination. Once they buy the property, they keep in mind how they'll maintain and renovate it. They understand the importance of doing deferred maintenance—repairing the roof, upgrading the sewage system, and so on. As they make a plan for the purchase, they're also planning for their overall ownership experience.

The Home Equity Factor

If you read the book *The Millionaire Next Door* by Drs. Thomas Stanley and William Danko, you'll find the millionaire they profile is typically the professional person or small business owner who makes only $60,000 or $70,000 per year. However, through a combination of spending conservatively and investing wisely, they've accumulated a net worth of a million dollars or more.

You can reach that attractive million-dollar milestone once you understand the importance of building equity in your real estate.

If you're not a high net worth individual, you probably have most of your equity in your primary residence. Over the last several years, the importance of building and maintaining equity in one's primary residence has been thrown out the window.

People have come to treat their homes as if they were an ATM. I'm certain this trend reflects today's incessant and pervasive marketing pitches. You've heard them: you need this car, you need this jewelry, you need these clothes, you need this trip.

The easy way to purchase these "goodies" is through a low-interest, easy-to-get home equity line of credit that you can access with a simple checkbook or debit card. Indeed, many banks and credit card companies send you blank checks in the mail. How easy. How enticing. How dangerous.

Imagine our grandparents or parents approving of you using a piece of plastic to go out and spend the equity you've gained in your home. Outrageous!

Don't Tap Long-Term Assets for Short-Term Buys

Luxury home buyers know the importance of maintaining the equity in their residence and don't tap into equity of their long-term assets such as real estate to buy things that depreciate. The most important thing a high net worth individual understands is this: *One should not use a long-term asset like real estate to finance the purchase of a short-term asset like a boat or car, or a vacation.*

Luxury buyers regard their homes as a capital asset, also termed a long-term asset. Increased equity in this asset involves creating a plan to pay off the financing as soon as possible and resisting the incessant marketing pitches to treat their home equity like their personal bank.

Those who repeatedly refinance their home to pull cash out in a rising market should have an "ATM" sign by their front doors instead of a house number.

I keep hearing about people who paid $300,000 or $400,000 for their homes, but now have mortgages of $500,000 or $600,000 because the home appreciated over time and they kept refinancing it to take out cash. The problems this creates become infinitely worse when overall home values decline, as they've been doing since 2008.

I had a neighbor who sold his company for a great price during the tech boom. It was a small local company, and he received a payout of just a bit more than eight figures.

Wealthy as he then was, he did not act like the luxury home buyer we are going to use as a model in this book. Every six months or so, he would come to me breathless with excitement over the latest bank appraisal on his home. I would ask him, "Why the appraisal?" He would reply that he had just refinanced again to pull money out. Each time, I would shake my head and say, "Are you crazy? You just sold your company for millions of dollars. Pay that mortgage off!"

My advice fell on deaf ears, and soon the house had been refinanced for far more than the purchase price. As his financial world fell apart around him, the house was repossessed by the bank—after it had begun swiftly deteriorating due to lack of upkeep and maintenance.

Another young friend quit his job at a well-known law firm to work for an Internet start up. Things went well at first up until the time the company went public.

He asked me what to do with his hard-earned windfall. Should he hold on to the stock or cash out? He was convinced that the stock had potential to increase even more. I advised him to sell enough to pay off the mortgage on his home, which he did.

Not too long after that, the company crashed and the remaining stock became worthless. Sad as it was, the fact that his home was paid off gave him breathing room as he searched for a new career.

In my career as a Real Estate agent, I've met numerous potential sellers who bought their homes at a high price and refinanced on a regular basis over the years. Now, they owe more than their houses are worth. Most can't understand why they can't sell them for more than the mortgage. They think it's unfair that they have negative equity. They basically "sold" their houses to the bank throughout the years, and have already received their money in the form of mortgage debt. That's the bottom line.

Treat Home Equity as Sacred

Luxury home buyers treat the equity in their homes as sacred, not like a cash machine. They let it grow in two ways: (1) through normal market appreciation, and (2) through paying off outstanding principal as quickly as they can afford to do so.

Luxury home buyers understand that appreciation doesn't always occur in a straight line—dips and valleys in values happen during the course of property ownership. But they also know that, except in extremely rare circumstances, real estate increases in value over the long-term.

One reason is that materials used in home construction—steel, wood, concrete, copper, even plastic—become more expensive every single year. You see this every time you purchase building materials at a store. And the skilled labor that home construction requires becomes more expensive every single year. The cost of everything that goes into your house will increase through time, and that will help build the equity. They would not interrupt that process by taking money from their equity to underwrite the purchase of short-term assets.

When would a luxury home buyer tap into the equity in a long-term capital asset? For an emergency such as paying for medical needs or for college tuition (one of the best investments you can make for yourself or members of your family).

Debt-Reduction Only One Time, Please

I almost hate to say this, but if you have a lot of high-interest credit card debt, it is okay to refinance your house one time to get rid of that debt. But only do it once to get back on track. After that, tear up those credit cards.

However, some people do this once, and then they fall off the wagon and do it again a second and third time. Discipline yourself so that you refinance your house only once to pay off high-interest credit card debt, and be sure you stick to that.

Let me reiterate this important point: The equity in your home—a long-term capital asset—should not be used for the purchase of a short-term asset or to cover an expense. It's like putting antique furniture in the fireplace to heat your home.

Secret #9: Action Plan

- Research the purchase of a home thoroughly.
- Use qualified experts to aid in home inspection and other research.
- Don't spend beyond your means just because you can initially afford it.
- Set aside funds for upkeep and repairs from the start.
- Don't use your home as if it were an ATM.
- Treat your home equity as sacred, tapping into it only for dire emergencies.

Secret #10: Luxury Home Buyers Study Value in the Marketplace

When referring to any real estate market, most people think in terms of *prices*—average price, median price, increasing and decreasing prices, and so on. In contrast, luxury home buyers think in terms of *value* in the marketplace. As discussed in Secret #6, they stay in tune with current home values through their networks.

Think about the guy driving his car in circles because he won't ask for directions. You rarely see high net worth individuals driving around and around. They stop and ask for directions, leaving their egos at the door to get the information they need to make intelligent, well-informed purchases that will enhance their financial future both in the short and long run.

As an example, they don't hesitate to get an appraisal or talk to the tax assessor about values as a function of assessments in the marketplace. They ask questions like, "Are sales prices running 10 percent under average tax assessments or 5 percent over?" Statistics like these are useful to know in the market you are investigating because they give you a basis or standard for comparing different properties.

After this type of questioning, you may discover that homes in your area of interest are selling on average for 105 percent of assessed value. This becomes a good benchmark when looking at property, especially if the seller wants a price that is 120 percent of assessment. The price could be on target, but further investigation is warranted. Be sure to find out why this offering price is outside the typical sales price of 105 percent of assessment.

Do High-End Home Buyers Ever Overpay?

Occasionally I see high net worth individuals overpaying for real estate, and I do mean occasionally. Luxury home buyers rarely throw money around. In a few cases, though, they rationalize overpaying for a property by saying, "I want this one. It suits my family's purposes exactly. I don't want to wait for something else to come on the market. I know I'm overpaying for this, but I don't care. I can afford it and I want it."

In contrast, the less affluent buyer often overpays for a property without realizing it. That's why, to understand value in the marketplace, it's crucial to talk to lenders, builders, and Real Estate professionals and ask:

- What does it cost to build a home similar to the one you are considering buying?
- What is the cost per square foot?
- How does that compare to the asking price of the home you want to buy?

Do your research by looking back at least six months, if not one or two years, for historic data on sales in the area that you're interested in. High-end home buyers understand value and they fine-tune their understanding by asking questions of anyone and everyone. They don't worry about how they look when they ask someone a question.

Add fun to your research and attend open houses in the selected area—a great way to get a feel for the market.

Secret #10: Action Plan

Research and choose a

- Lender
- Builder
- Appraiser
- Prepare your list of questions for these professionals. Your questions may include but should not be limited to:
- What are current mortgage rates and requirements for pre-approval?
- What is the cost per square foot to build a home similar to the one you are contemplating?
- Are property values stable, increasing, or decreasing?
- How long are properties staying on the market?
- What is the average time on the market?
- Do your research by looking back at least six months (ideally, one or two years) for historic data on sales.
- Identify and attend three to five open houses on the next Saturday and Sunday to build your base of knowledge.

Luxury home buyers look at the big picture—the property, the location, and the utility it offers themselves and their family. They know the family goals for the purchase of this property and they know if the property will meet them.

They don't major in minor details, like worrying about a missing half bath when their goal is to have a south-facing property on the water with a nice beach so they can go fishing and swimming with their grandchildren.

Unlike the luxury home buyer, home buyers in lower price ranges can get hung up on details like whether the exterior of a home is made of clapboard instead of shingle, or determining the "R" value of the bulkhead. Some even spend a lot of time measuring the insides of closets.

That's not big-picture thinking—it's focusing on minor things in the context of making the biggest purchase in their lives.

Most Important Big-Picture Factor

What's the most important big-picture factor to consider in buying a property? Location.

When assessing the location of a home you might want to buy, ask these questions:

- Is this the best location I can afford?
- Will this location maximize the lifestyle my family and I desire?

- Is this the best location within the neighborhood I've selected?

No Perfect House

I know of a luxury home owner who purchased a summer estate and began a renovation project that lasted nearly two years and cost in the millions of dollars. When the project was complete, he wasn't satisfied with the outcome, tore the house down, and started over with a new plan.

What's the lesson? No matter how much money you have to invest, there is no perfect house. You have to determine what degree of "perfect" will satisfy you!

To major in big-picture thinking, you might have to compromise on details like not having a finished basement because you know that, to have that feature, you'd have to compromise on location. Don't sacrifice this key big-picture factor.

If you want a home in an older, more established part of town, you might find you have to settle for a home with less square footage. That would be a valid decision based on a big-picture consideration.

Consider others factors, too, such as possibly having a wet basement at certain times of the year, having a nuisance neighbor (e.g., a commercial property or nearby highway), or having a house with an out-of-place or otherwise unappealing style.

If the home you are looking at is burdened with any of these, think long and hard about moving forward. In fact, buying it only makes sense if you can get a spectacular deal that will enable you to price it substantially under the market when you sell it. Be prepared—you could have this home on the market for a long time.

What Can and Can't Be Changed

Luxury home buyers understand the difference between the things they can and can't change, and the importance of making this distinction.

If a property has the location, privacy, and orientation they are looking for, they won't be concerned if it has electric heating instead of gas or oil. In fact, the luxury home buyer will recognize opportunity in purchasing the house that has electric heat. Because of the stigma electric heat has in many markets, he or she may negotiate a reduction in price that surpasses the cost of replacing it.

Location can't be changed and views can't be created for any price. Smaller details *can* be changed, so they should be kept in perspective.

You can always add bigger windows, renovate the kitchen or baths, add a bath, or finish off the basement. But you can't change the location, orientation, or the view, and you can't always easily create privacy. These are the big-picture items that the high-end luxury home buyer focuses on when purchasing property.

Secret #11: Action Plan

- Focus on the most important, big-picture factor: Location.
- Don't sweat the small details like windows, flooring, or color schemes because they can always be changed. What primarily can't be changed are location, views, and privacy.

Secret #12:
Luxury Home Buyers Apply Three Key Negotiation Strategies

Luxury home buyers don't like to feel "outgunned" when negotiating the purchase or sale of real estate. After all, these folks are often doing million- or billion-dollar deals as part of their daily business activities.

Most people hate to feel overpowered in any negotiation, but they often do feel that way when making large-ticket purchases such as a car, and especially a home. No one enjoys that feeling of powerlessness—that "I'm about to be taken" feeling.

Three Strategies

Throughout the years, I've studied negotiation extensively by reading multiple books, listening to recordings, and attending seminars near and far on the subject. Harvard Law School and Massachusetts Institute of Technology (MIT) are among the many institutions offering fantastic negotiation seminars that I've attended.

Based on everything I've experienced and learned throughout three decades in the Real Estate business, I share the following three strategies to guide you through negotiations successfully:

1. Negotiate from a standpoint of confidence.
2. Don't assume you know the needs of the other party.
3. Detach from the outcome.

Let's examine each of these strategies in detail to learn how they can be applied to the process of negotiating a real estate purchase.

1. Strive for Confidence

The website Dictionary.com defines confidence as: "full trust; belief in the powers, trustworthiness, or reliability of a person or thing" or "belief in oneself and one's powers or abilities; self-confidence; self-reliance; assurance."

If you put into action all the strategies and techniques laid out in this book, I guarantee that, over time, you will attain a level of confidence in purchasing real estate. Even with poor negotiation abilities, the confident buyer frequently prevails over the skilled but non-confident seller because people accede to those they perceive have power.

Becoming confident in your market—knowing about pricing, sales histories, and so on— is a journey and not necessarily a destination. If you expect to become confident overnight, you're not being realistic. Learning negotiation skills takes time.

On the other hand, you don't want to be looking at Real Estate ads three months from now, realizing you've not taken any steps toward your goal of gaining knowledge in your desired market to help build your confidence.

If you've begun taking action, congratulations. You're on your way to becoming a confident buyer. You will gain competence, and thus confidence, each day you work on your plan.

2. Make No Assumptions

In the process of negotiation, people frequently get in trouble by assuming certain "facts."

Assuming you know the needs of another party often takes you on a nonproductive course of action. In response, the person you're negotiating with digs into his or her position. Negotiating from an unwavering position can be frustrating and fruitless. People who do it often find themselves in stalemate situations and in a terrible mood. In this situation, they rarely achieve the outcome they seek.

It's natural to make assumptions based on one's own values and biases. For example, you might say you like fast cars. I might then assume you like Porsches, while, in fact, all convertibles feel fast to you. You might say you want a home with privacy. I might then assume you mean four acres in the middle of nowhere, while your definition of privacy is a half acre framed with evergreens.

Similarly, be careful not to base your perceptions of the other party's position on your own beliefs and values.

Peel Back the Layers

Don't assume you know the needs of the other party, and don't assume that his or her needs are exactly as stated. For example, a seller takes the position of being willing to close only in the month of June. Another seller will offer to sell only for 100 percent of the asking price. As soon as one party in a negotiation gets stuck, the other party to the negotiation often digs deeper into his or her position and the head-butting begins. What results? A stalemate.

Therefore, to emulate the skilled luxury real estate negotiator, you'd peel back the layers and look beyond the other's "stuck" position to understand (not assume) the person's true needs.

In the case of a seller insisting on a closing date in June, you may inquire and find out that the date coincides with the availability of the home the seller is moving to. If you need to close by May 1 because your mortgage interest rate will expire after that date, you could offer to let the seller stay on for a month after the closing to avoid losing your rate.

The bottom line is the need to fact-find carefully by asking questions so you can be sure you understand the needs of the other party. Only then do you have a chance to craft a solution that meets those needs. Working on solutions based on any *assumptions* of their needs will only lead to frustration.

For instance, as an agent, I know that if a buyer says he or she wants a property that offers complete privacy from neighbors, I (relying on my own belief or value system) might assume the buyer wants a property with several acres. Further probing might lead to something different, like a special "jewel" of a property in an area where small lots are normal but homes are totally contained within walls, and year-round landscaping gives them privacy.

Likewise, when you're not working from the same definitions as your negotiation counterparts, it's easy to make incorrect assumptions. Always check them out!

When you are dealing with a seller who will accept 100 percent of the asking price *only*, you might be required to peel even more layers off the metaphorical onion. Perhaps this seller is insecure or hopes to pay off his or her high credit card debt with the sale proceeds. Or perhaps this is an ego-driven person who needs to look intelligent and can't negotiate what appears to be a great deal.

You'll only find the seller's motivation by asking lots of questions, either directly or through the seller's agent. "Mr. Seller, we are still not in agreement on a selling price for your property. It would be helpful for me to know how you arrived at the price for your home. Perhaps I'm missing some key market data." You would be astounded at how truthful many sellers are in replying, just as we speculated at the beginning of this paragraph. The seller might reply, "My credit card balances are pretty high and I am moving to a more expensive area." They may or may not answer this directly, but you'll never know until you ask.

Once you fully understand the other person's needs, you can respond by sharing market evidence on the extraordinary value contained in this transaction. Perhaps you will present data on the cost to reproduce a home similar to the one you are working to purchase or other market-based evidence to allow this position-focused person to feel as if he or she has won.

This is where your research comes into play to help your negotiation.

3. Detach from the Outcome

If you learn nothing else in negotiating, learn to detach from the outcome. Why? Because excessive attachment can allow the negotiation process to drift into position-based negotiating rather than need-based negotiating.

When negotiating, high net worth individuals want the other party to know that they aren't desperate to complete the deal. Learn from this and always be willing to walk away. Sometimes you'll have to.

In the process of negotiating your real estate purchase, you can use the strategy of detaching from the outcome by having other purchase alternatives to pursue should negotiations on the particular one you are working on not come together. Most important, you need to let the seller know you have other options and that *you* are not "attached" to the outcome of owning this particular home.

In the End

By using each of these three strategies of negotiation—building confidence, avoiding making assumptions, and detaching from the outcome—you will greatly increase your chances of negotiating a favorable purchase of a home at a fair price.

Presenting Offers

Here's an example, from an agent's perspective, of how I presented offers to a local builder of luxury second homes who had high ego needs and was a classic position negotiator. To make matters even more challenging, this particular builder-seller always wanted his properties to sell for more money than had ever been realized in the marketplace. His aggressive pricing made it difficult to obtain an offer, and when an offer did come in, his first reaction was expressed in words that can't be stated in print.

I finally learned the concept of detaching from the outcome, and it changed my whole approach to presenting offers to this builder. When one came in (and it was always low because his prices were always high), I would simply say to him, "I received an offer on the property at Bay Road." Before he could utter a response, I would say, "I need your authorization to reject the offer."

"Well, how much is the offer?" he would ask.

"It's low," I would reply, "and I need your authorization to reject it. I can't reject offers without your authorization."

We would do two or three rounds of this when finally, in frustration, he'd scream at me. "How much is the offer?"

So, more often than not, when I stated the amount of the offer, he'd say, "Well, that's not as low as I thought. We can work with that." A counteroffer and different attitude followed. This meant he could say he was "saving a deal," which was great for his ego.

In asking for permission to reject the offer before actually disclosing its contents, I provided the ultimate signal of detachment from the outcome. This broadcasted the message that I was not pushing the seller into accepting an offer I knew was less than what he wanted (which would have insulted his ego), even though it may have been a fair offer in the current market.

What's In It For Me?

When negotiating purchase price, never use position as the reason for making your counteroffer. When you tell a seller that $400,000 is "the highest number I will go for this property," then you might as well kiss that transaction goodbye.

Rather than holding a position, always frame negotiations in the context of WIIFM (What's In It For Me). In this example, a better way to reply to the seller is to say, "Based on marketplace knowledge, comparable sales, and competing properties currently available, I am willing to offer $400,000 for your property." In other words, talk about the market, not about an unmovable position. Remember, sellers only care about what is important to *them*. This would *not* include the fact that you have set a limit of X or can only afford the amount you offered. By bringing the discussion back to the market, you're speaking to their interest—that is, how the market values the property and not how you, in your own self-interest, value it. This scenario allows you to see how this process could apply to any negotiation as you carefully build a meaningful foundation for becoming a successful real estate purchaser.

Secret #12: Action Plan

Create a negotiation plan:

- Use market data to determine what price the market will support for the home you are considering.
- Do research to determine what it would cost to rebuild that home.
- Write out your negotiating points in terms of "WIIFM," using the data on price and building cost.
- Employ the three strategies: strive for confidence, don't make assumptions, and detach from the outcome as you determine your "walk-away" factors (i.e., at what price, terms, or conditions you would walk away from this transaction).

Jack Cotton started his Real Estate company in his college dormitory room thirty-five years ago and remains in Real Estate to this day. He didn't need to work for another broker to learn the business because he "knew it all" at the age of twenty-one. In fact, he knew so much that it took him one year, two months, and three weeks to sell his first house.

Things improved, though, and over the next three decades, Cotton Real Estate became one of the most admired and professional Real Estate companies on Cape Cod.

Jack sold Cotton Real Estate to Sotheby's International Realty in 2005. Agents at this firm continue to post the highest per-person sales on the Cape.

Jack transitioned away from sales toward growing, running, and managing the firm's Cape Cod offices, while working with high net worth clients. Since this acquisition, he has opened three new offices for Sotheby's International Realty.

Over the years, Jack has been involved in nearly every record-breaking luxury residential sale on Cape Cod, either directly as the agent or as coach to the agent involved.

In the fall of 2008, he stepped down as manager and has returned to being an agent while developing educational products.

His first book, *A Dog's Guide to Life: Lessons from "Moose,"* is in its second printing. Available at most bookstores and Amazon.com, it offers valuable insights to both the personal and business side of life.

Appendix A

Reading List

---

100 Questions Every First-Time Home Buyer Should Ask: With Answers from Top Brokers from Around the Country, by Ilyce R. Glink.

The 106 Common Mistakes Homebuyers Make (and How to Avoid Them), by Gary W. Eldred.

Tips and Traps When Buying a Home (Tips & Traps), by Robert Irwin (Paperback—Dec. 17, 2008).

The National Association of Realtors Guide to Home Buying, by National Association of Realtors (NAR) and Blanche Evans

The Millionaire Next Door: The Surprising Secrets of America's Wealthy, by Thomas J. Stanley and William D. Danko.

Stop Acting Rich . . . And Start Living Like A Real Millionaire, by Thomas J. Stanley.

Rich Dad, Poor Dad: What the Rich Teach Their Kids About Money—That the Poor and Middle Class Do Not!, by Robert T. Kiyosaki and Sharon L. Lechter.

The Total Money Makeover: A Proven Plan for Financial Fitness, by Dave Ramsey.

Getting to Yes: Negotiating Agreement Without Giving In, by Roger Fisher, William L. Ury, and Bruce Patton.

See You at the Top: 25th Anniversary Edition, by Zig Ziglar.

Think and Grow Rich, by Napoleon Hill.

Goals! How to Get Everything You Want—Faster Than You Ever Thought Possible, by Brian Tracy.

Free Download
of the net worth tracking spreadsheet featured in this book.

Total Value - $57.00
Yours free at www.JackCotton.com

Click Down Loads
Enter Password
Spreadsheets will be sent back as an email attachment

Share Your Story

I hope you put the ideas and strategies in this book to use in finding your dream home starting today.

Send me your success stories,
home purchasing ideas and comments.

jack@jackcotton.com

You never know, you might be included in a future book or program!

Jack Cotton
851 Main Street
P. O. Box 68
Osterville, MA 02655
508.957.5500
jack@jackcotton.com
www.jackcotton.com